Learn To Handle Trauma Like A Champion

Recovering From Traumatic Events

Sensei Paul David

Copyright Page

Learn To Handle Trauma Like A Champion:
Recovering From Traumatic Events,
by Sensei Paul David

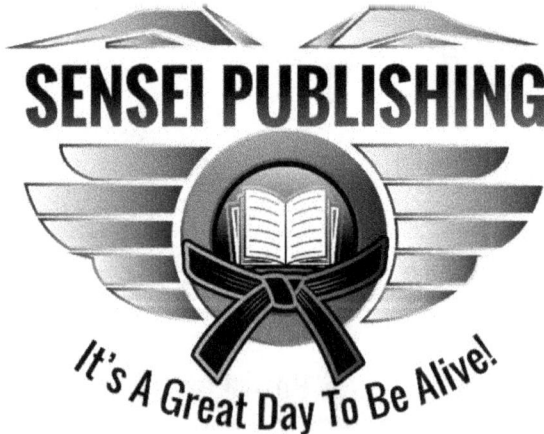

SENSEI PUBLISHING

It's A Great Day To Be Alive!

www.senseipublishing.com

@senseipublishing
#senseipublishing

Get/Share Our FREE All-Ages Mental Health Book Now!

FREE Self-Development Book for Every Family

Click Below or Search Amazon for Another Book In This Series

Join Our Publishing Journey!

If you would like to receive FUTURE FREE BOOKS and get to know us better, please click www.senseipublishing.com and join our newsletter by entering your email address in the pop-up box.

Follow Our Blog: senseipauldavid.ca

Follow/Like/Subscribe: Facebook, Instagram, YouTube: @senseipublishing

Scan the QR Code with your phone or tablet

to follow us on social media: Like / Subscribe / Follow

Thank You from The Author: Sensei Paul David

Before we dive in, I would like to thank you for picking up this book from among the many other similar books out there. Thank you for choosing to invest in my book. That means everything to me.

Now that you are here, I ask you to stick with me as we take your self-discovery journey together. I promise to make our time together valuable and worthwhile.

In the pages ahead, you will find some areas of information and practices more helpful than others - and that is great! I encourage you to apply what works best for you. You will benefit from the knowledge that you gain and the ensuing exciting transformation of character.

Enjoy!

Contents

Foreword

We have all experienced traumatic events in one way or the other. Nonetheless, the intensity, implication, and impact they have on each of us are not the same. Some people seem to find it easier to recover from unpleasant experiences than others. What is the cause of these differences? Are they due to our genetic makeup? You will find out the answer in *Learn To Handle Trauma Like A Champion.*

This is a timely book compiled by Paul to help people struggling to recover from traumatic experiences, with research-based principles. The meticulousness involved in crafting this material is commendable and should be used as a blueprint for new authors.

It is precise and to the point, without fluff and esoteric principles that are found in some similar material. This material is full of proven tips that have helped many individuals get their lives on track. I hope it will be as valuable to you as it has been to me.

Introduction

"Trauma is hell on earth. Trauma resolved is a gift from the gods."

Peter A. Levine

This is not the first time I am writing a book. I have been privileged to write a number of books, and it is possible that you are reading this material because of my previous works. Yet, I can tell you that this project is special to me. I have had firsthand experience of what it means to suffer from traumatic experiences. So, I feel so privileged to be able to contribute my quota to your journey.

In the last few years, I have met various people who have been victims of abusive interpersonal and professional relationships. The impact of such events lingers, and they ruin the victims' happiness. I have been privileged to help several people walk through their experience and helped put their lives back on track.

Their new lease on life after recovery is my inspiration for writing this book. I have taken it upon myself to include many quotes from survivors of traumatic experiences to add a personal touch. I can imagine that this material will give you the inspiration and help you need to experience the adrenaline rush of happiness and motivation again. Today is a good day to be alive!

Chapter One:
What You Need To Know
About Trauma

"Most of us have unhealthy thoughts and emotions that have either developed as a result of trauma or hardships in our childhood or the way we were raised."

Steven Seagal

It is better to read about trauma than to experience it because it is not a pleasant experience. Many do not know how to handle it. Only a few get the help they need. Unfortunately, instead of getting the support they need from their friends and family, some people get stigmatized, further complicating the issue for them. We will start this journey by dissecting this phenomenon.

Facts About Trauma

I could have named this section "Interesting facts about trauma," but the reality is that there is nothing exciting or interesting about this issue. People who experience it do not find it amusing in any way. Yet, it is important to understand some important facts about trauma to enable you to deal with it. I need to warn you that you are about to be exposed to some uncomfortable statistics regarding trauma.

Yet, we need this section to help you understand why you need to take this issue seriously and act as speedily, before things get out of hand! The institution responsible and committed to helping people recover from traumatic events in the US is the American Association for the Surgery of Trauma. Below are some things you need to know about this issue; according to this organization:

Trauma Is An Illness

Unknown to many people, they think trauma is just one of those things we face as human beings. Meanwhile, it is actually an illness. Note though, that the fact that a person remembers an unpleasant event and it affects them, does not mean that they are necessarily ill..

However, it is a mental health issue when it is recurrent in such a way that it impairs the ability of the person to carry out their daily activities. At that point, the person is experiencing what is known as Post-Traumatic Stress Disorder (PTSD), which is a serious mental health issue.

Trauma Is A Killer

Among adults of up to 45 years of age in the US, trauma is the leading cause of death! That makes it a serious matter! In the overall category, it is the fourth leading cause of death in the US. Note that trauma, by itself, cannot kill a person.

Yet, it can lead to various complications, such as an amplification of a physical health condition. It can also lead to suicidal ideation at its peak, leading to the death of many people around the world. Therefore, this is not an issue you can treat with levity because it has destructive tendencies.

Trauma Is An Economic Problem

According to the American Association for the Surgery of Trauma, the estimated cost of trauma globally is $518 billion. This health issue affects the finances of both individuals and governments of countries around the world. Trauma is categorized into two types – Big T and Little T.

Big T is trauma caused by major events, such as natural disasters, wars, car accidents, or sexual assault. Meanwhile, Little t is trauma from events such as an unexpected relocation or divorce. Either way, traumatic occurrences take their toll on the health and personal lives of people in such a way that they affect their finances.

Trauma Can Be Defeated

The most important fact about trauma you need to understand is that it can be defeated. Regardless of the intensity and difficulties you can experience due to a traumatic event, the good news is that you can recover from it. According to trauma statistics, 46% of people dealing with this health issue recover after just six weeks of psychotherapy.

So, there is no cause for alarm if you have been battling trauma for years. In most cases, the only reason you have not recovered is the fact that you have decided to get stuck in the rut. You have turned your trauma into your identity, making it challenging for you to change the status quo.

Post-Traumatic Stress Disorder

As stated earlier, trauma is not classified as an illness until it progresses to the PTSD stage. Post-Traumatic Stress Disorder is a mental health issue that occurs as a result of exposure to an intensely unpleasant experience. People dealing with this issue struggle to eat, sleep and have a normal life as a result of exposure to events such as fatal accidents, major natural disasters, wars, or rape.

It was an issue that was common among war veterans, but things are different in the modern world. Before now, people had to experience wars and other traumatic events to battle PTSD. However, in recent times, some individuals now experience this issue due to their uncontrolled social medial affinity. Exposure to traumatic videos on social media can give you a similar feeling to the people who experience the events first-hand. Thus, it is essential that you are careful while surfing the internet.

It Is Never Easy For Women

Women are most affected by this mental health issue, especially when it is in the form of a divorce or war. This reality is understandable. For example, in a divorce, women usually have more to lose than men. Society typically frowns on single women, especially when they have gone through a divorce. The stigma is unreal in such a way that it can unsettle them and make it challenging for them to recover.

Besides, if the woman had been assaulted and brutalized while living with the man, it can be difficult for them to forget such experiences. In some cases, the fear of the man is instilled in them such that they are scared that he might come back to hurt them again. The fear of being brutalized can make them stay indoors and the difficulty of raising children alone can make it hard for them to get their lives together again after the separation.

Thankfully, legal practitioners are aware of these challenges and often do their best to help such women get a large enough settlement from such cases. Women that have experienced wars, also have sad tales to tell. Some of them lose their husbands and children and are sometimes victims of rape during that period. So, recovering from such events is never easy for anyone. In all, it is best to avoid traumatic experiences, if at all possible. Yet, when you find yourself in this situation, there is a way out.

Chapter Two:
The Issue Is Real!

"After a traumatic experience, the human system of self-preservation seems to go onto permanent alert as if the danger might return at any moment."

Judith Lewis

One of the reasons some people struggle to recover from traumatic events is that they try to sweep the issue under the carpet. Sometimes, they do this hoping that they will somehow heal from the issue over time. However, despite their good intentions, pretending that the event is not a problem will inhibit their recovery. In this chapter, we will discuss the importance of facing the fact to recover from traumatic events.

A Change Of Perspective

According to Mark Goulston, MD, trauma changes your perspective on life, and that is why you notice that you are no longer the same afterward. If it is not real, why has it changed your worldview? This is the question you need to ask yourself. You can detect that you are living in denial when you experience the following change in your perspective after a traumatic experience:

You Stop Trusting Others

One of the common signs of a failure to recover from a traumatic event is that you stop trusting others. You become paranoid because you do not want to be hurt again. Of course, there is nothing wrong with being careful. It is normal that you do not want to repeat the same mistake. In fact, it is a sign of intelligence when you put measures in place that ensure that you do not experience the same kind of hurt.

However, you can do it incorrectly. When some people are hurt, they make generalized statements such as "all men are evil." The fact that a man hurt you as a woman does not mean that there are no good men out there. At least, I am a good man! (That's on a lighter note.) The point is that you do not have to generalize because you are hurt. If you refuse to trust everyone, you will struggle to turn things around.

You Prefer To Be Alone

At some point in our lives, we will prefer to be alone. In fact, it is recommended that you have periods in your day when you are alone so that you can reflect and plan for the future. It is a sign of an intelligent mind. However, it is problematic when you prefer to be alone a lot, especially after a traumatic event. It is not a good sign.

One of the symptoms of depression is withdrawal. Of course, you might want to take time to yourself so that you can process the event and recover. Nonetheless, it is risky when you do not want your friends and family to stay around you during this period. If you discover that you always prefer to stay alone and withdraw from social activities for a prolonged period after an unpleasant experience, it is a sign that you are still hurting.

You Hate The World

Indeed, the world is full of evil, and there are many things to dislike about the modern world. Yet, there are also many things to love about the world. So, the fact that you have had distasteful experiences does not in any way invalidate the fact that the world is a beautiful place. Do not allow negative experiences to cloud your judgment to the point where they make you regret the fact that you are alive.

The fact that you hate the world after a traumatic experience is a conspicuous indication that you are yet to recover from the experience. Remember that there is light at the end of the tunnel. Sunshine comes after the rain. The fact that you are in a period of your life, full of sad events, does not mean that you will not experience bliss and fulfillment in the future. Keep the faith!

You Find Fault Easily

The paranoia that comes from the absence of recovery after a traumatic event often leads to the tendency to be quick to judge others. After some people have experienced a divorce, they stop believing in love, making thembelieve that true love does not exist.

Whenever they see a man displaying affection towards a woman, they assume that it is yet another scam. They generally become negative towards any man, which makes them often quick to say disgusting things about others. For such people, no one seems to have the right intention from that point forward in their lives. If this is your experience, it is a sign that you need to recover from your past hurt.

You Bully Others

The shameless and unreasonable decision of online bullies is a sign that many people are hurting in this world. Instead of them seeking help and recovering, they prefer to hate others and bully them online. Social media platforms are perfect places for bullying behavior because you can easily hide behind your phone and make disgusting comments. You can even create an anonymous account for that purpose, and people are hardly ever prosecuted for their comments online.

If you notice that you have a burning desire to make others sad with your comments online, it is a sign that you need to heal from a previous wound. Some people say harsh things towards others online, unprovoked. This unreasonable behavior often comes from people that are hurting and that have chosen to unleash their anger on others. This is not the right approach. Instead, choose to heal.

Choose To Heal

Unless you choose to heal, your life will continue to revolve around a circle of negativity. At some point, even your friends and family will start avoiding you. No one wants to stay around negative people. Therefore, do not be surprised that your loved ones are avoiding you when you allow the stench of negativity to consume you. Your paranoia will extend to them at some point and no one wants that.

If your resentment, bitterness, and lack of trust linger, you will only surround yourself with negative people, which is not good for your mental health. It is time to move on. It is time to try something new. Open up yourself for mental surgery that will change your life. You can only get help when you decide that you are ready to heal. The journey will be challenging but will be worth it eventually.

Chapter Three:
Wrong Techniques Of
Recovering From Trauma

"Delusional pain hurts just as much as the pain from actual trauma. So, what if it's all in your head?"

Tracy Morgan

Instead of finding a solution to their issues, some people only end up further complicating matters for themselves. If you let trauma overwhelm you, the product can be disastrous. It can make you cause pain to others before eventually hurting yourself. It is never worth it. In this chapter, we will discuss some counterproductive methods people use to deal with trauma, so that you can avoid them.

The Don'ts Of Recovery From Trauma

The following approaches will not help you build resilience or recover from traumatic events:

Denial

You will never make any attempt to recover from a traumatic event as long as you keep denying that it hurts. Understandably, this is usually the first stage of grief, as theorized by Bowlby and Parkes. You are surprised that such a thing happened, leading to numbness and shock. Yet, it is not healthy to remain in this stage for too long. Time does not automatically change situations unless you are deliberate about turning things around.

Denial will prevent you from exposing yourself to the help you need to recover and get yourself back on track. No one will be able to help you if you keep denying that you need to solve a problem. In some cases, the reason people choose this approach is that they are afraid of opening the wound afresh. They do not want to be exposed to the vulnerabilities that come with remembering and dealing with the issue. So, they prefer to pretend that they are not hurt any longer.

Bitterness

Even people that admit that they are hurt are sometimes bitter because of the event. They remember how they were treated like trash and ended up hating the perpetrator. They curse and wish something bad would happen to the person as though that would placate them. The reality is that the deed is done. So, wishing the person evil will not change the situation even if your wish comes to pass.

As long as you are bitter, you will not be able to recover from the issue. Meanwhile, research has established a link between forgiveness and well-being. People who choose to forgive, often have happier and more meaningful lives afterward. Refusing to forgive a person will only block your own path to healing from your hurt. Unforgiveness is like a cancer that prevents your wound from healing. Let it go for your sake, and take a different approach to be able to enjoy the happy and fulfilled life you crave.

Vengeance

One of the natural products of bitterness and resentment is vengeance. When you hate a person, you wish something bad would happen to them, and when it is not forthcoming, you might be tempted to take matters into your own hands. The best you can do if you want justice is to report the case to the police and get what you deserve in the law court, especially if you have evidence to prove your case.

However, if you are not willing to explore that channel as a result of factors such as the absence of evidence, it is best that you let it go. The truth about life is that evil peoples' lives often end badly. However, it is best that you do not try to make them pay by using violent means. This approach can get you in trouble. If you injure or kill someone in the process, you might be prosecuted and lose your freedom or your life. So, it is definitely never the best approach to handling trauma.

Blaming Others

It is true that some people play critical roles in hurting others. For example, an abusive husband is responsible for the trauma experienced by his wife afterward. Also, the evil person that raped a woman is responsible for the trauma the female experiences after the event. Yet, no one is responsible for how you live your life in the aftermath of a seriously unpleasant event. Never allow the madness of one person to determine your future.

Do not deny the damage to your life that was done by other people. Still, you have the ability to make the most of your life. It is easy to blame others for your misfortunes because it absolves you from the pressure of striving to achieve success. You might have been wronged by insensitive people who betrayed you, but it is within your power to turn your life around and make it a source of inspiration to others.

Rejecting Help

Of course, you cannot accept the help of every Tom, Dick, and Harry because some people have ulterior motives for helping others. Some people offer to help so that they can control the person or make that individual do their bidding in the future. Some men help women so that they can, in return, ask them for sex in the future. So, it is understandable that you are being careful about getting help from others.

Yet, it is not advisable to reject the help of others when recovering from a traumatic event, especially when they do not have a history of asking you for favors in return. According to Michael Imperioli, "When you are going through these difficult times of chaos and trauma, the most important thing is to keep those who are closest to you together." If you have friends and family that can help you, be open enough to receive their help. We all need all the help we can get in our low times.

Silence

Silence is not always golden. M.B. Dallocchio noted that some people who experienced traumatic events, especially veterans, wish they could open up to others, but no one wants to listen to them. On the other hand, some individuals prefer to keep things to themselves, but they have people pestering them to talk. It is quite unfortunate that some people will not give their loved ones the attention they need, for them to share the things that hurt them.

If you are fortunate enough to have friends and family willing to listen to you, do not hesitate to speak to them about your pain. Speaking to others is a form of therapy used in psychology, known as psychotherapy or talking analysis. It was championed by psychologist Sigmund Freud. Make the most of such opportunities. Silence is never the best approach. It will only make your pain slowly kill you.

Chapter Four:
You Can Do It Also

"Once we believe in ourselves, we can risk curiosity, wonder, spontaneous delight, or any experience that reveals the human spirit."

E. E. Cummings

Starting with this chapter, we will be dealing with proven techniques that can help you recover from traumatic events. We will start by encouraging you to trust yourself to handle the situation before introducing you to the stories of some people that recovered after experiencing unpleasant situations. I hope their stories will inspire you to start your journey.

Face The Fact

"As soon as you trust yourself, you will know how to live."

Johann Wolfgang von Goethe

In order to heal, you need to trust yourself. Of course, this can be challenging to do, especially if you are convinced that it was your mistake that landed you in trouble in the first place. Yet, you need to believe that you have what it takes to turn things around. Admit that the issue is real and recognize your need to heal.

Shun every tendency to deny that you are hurting and get set to face your demons. Once you make up your mind to turn things around, the problem is partially solved. The truth is that your situation is not unique. Other people have had the same experience or even worse and recovered from it. You deserve some sunshine!

Learning From Others

The moment you find people that have recovered from similar experiences, it weakens your defense and makes you vulnerable enough for the healing process. Below are some people that have experienced traumatic events but chose to be positive and make the best out of their lives:

Will Smith

We all make mistakes. Don't we? Indeed, it was wrong of Will Smith to have slapped Chris Rock, especially in an event as publicized as the Oscar Academy Award. Yet, the fact that he came out to apologize for his actions shows what the man is about. It was a rare moment of madness for a man that is loved around the world for his dazzling performance in movies such as King Richard, Aladdin, and The Fresh Prince of Bel-Air.

Unknown to many people, this man has not always had it easy. He had an alcoholic father who was physically abusive toward his mother and family. He hated him so much that he contemplated killing him. Yet, he grew up with the intention to spread love around the world, which is usually the theme of most movies he stars in. Despite his flaws, it is evident that he is a man that has refused to allow his past to determine his future.

Oprah Winfrey

Anyone going through tough periods in their life should know the story of this self-made millionaire. Things could have gone any way for her after she was sexually abused as a child and also got pregnant when she was just fourteen! For some people, such experiences would have given them reason to become sexual perverts and hate the world. Not Oprah.

She is famous for her unreal empathy toward her guests on her talk show. No one would have blamed her if she had failed in life and become a disaster. However, she opted to heal. She faced her demons and made the best out of her life. Many people today want to replicate her success without the awareness that she came a long way from poverty and trauma.

Eminem

Marshall Matters is a strong personality, and the intensity of his raps lends credence to that. He is the favorite rapper of many people around the world and has achieved remarkable success in his career. Nonetheless, Eminem would have preferred a better childhood.

His father was never there for him, and his mother was as unstable as a reed on water. She moved around frequently, partly due to her suffering from Munchausen by Proxy Syndrome. He was often the victim of bullies who frequently physically assaulted him. Yet, he chose to put his pain into lyrics rather than weaponize it to ruin others.

NF

Rapper Nathan John Feuerstein has a lot of similarities to Eminem. The first is the intensity of their raps. Interestingly, Eminem has a half-brother, named Nathan, which often makes people wonder if the two are related. Besides, they both had traumatic childhoods. NF was often bullied as a kid, and his mother died from drug abuse.

He wrote a song to describe the anguish, and he was literally crying as he rapped about it. However, despite his difficult childhood, NF has chosen to put his pain into his songs to help others in similar situations heal from their hurt.

Charlize Theron

Actress Charlize Theron is the darling of many people with her distinct ability to interpret her roles perfectly. However, her teenage years were full of trauma as she watched her mom shoot and kill her father right in front of her! That's some story, isn't it?

That's not something you come across every day. Well, this is the story: her father often physically assaulted her mother, which eventually led to her mother shooting him in an act of self-defense. Yet, that is not something you want to witness as a teenager.

Christina Aguilera

The television personality has made a name for herself with her four-octave vocal range, but young Christina was only six years old when her parents divorced. Her father emotionally and physically assaulted her mother until she could no longer take it, which led to the dissolution of the marriage.

No one wants to start their lives on this note because the sad reality often lingers.

Besides, children with problematic childhoods often grow up into maladaptive adults. Yet, in the case of Christina, she handled it well, and fortunately, she is doing well for herself now.

Benjamin Graham

Unlike most of the people on this list, Benjamin's trauma did not come from being physically or emotionally abused. Rather, it was a product of his huge loss from his investments in the time of the Great Depression. Warren Buffet's mentor could have given up on investing and tried something else.

Instead, he chose to learn from the failure and used the lessons to become a better investor and a mentor to many new-age investors. What a man! Long after his demise, his books remain blueprints for new investors.

Chapter Five:
Reviewing The Event

"There is no timestamp on trauma. There isn't a formula that you can insert yourself into to get from horror to healing. Take your space. Let your journey be the balm."

Dawn Serra

Experts recommend recasting an event to make it lose its sting. This technique is useful in various ways. People use it to deal with procrastination by perceiving a challenging task as a task you need to understand. You can apply this method when trying to recover from traumatic events. This chapter will teach you how to go about it.

Take The Tough Walk

In *The Body Keeps The Score,* author Bessel van der Kolk, M.D., proceeded todescribe the experience of a boy who witnessed the horror of the events of 9/11. According to the author, the child was not traumatized by the exposure partly because he grew up in a supportive and loving family. He opined that the major factor for the seemingly superhuman ability of the boy to recover from the experience is the fact that he took productive action by "running away" from the events in his mind.

He explained that the boy is able to process his experience through the power of imagination, which involves making drawings of what he saw. The author explained that people who are traumatized have a culture of organizing their lives in a way that makes them feel like the traumatic experience continues. This practice sets up such people to live their lives in such a way that makes them relive the experience all over again, stirring up negative emotions regularly. Bessel recommends that we all need to develop a mechanism or strategy like the boy that enables us to run away from the emotions of the event.

Take Out The Sting

The way you process a past event determines whether it will continue to hurt or not. What is your conclusion after thinking about what happened? Your response will affect how you feel when you recollect the event. The following strategies will help you to process traumatic experiences in such a way that you will remove their ability to hurt you:

Gratitude

Gratitude is more than a practice; it is an attitude. It is a deliberate decision to find the silver lining in a bad situation. Some people assume that you can only be grateful when things are in your favor. Anyone can be grateful when things are moving in the right direction. However, it takes a mature mind to find reasons to be thankful when things are not going as planned. They ask, "Why should I be grateful after this divorce?"

Of course, you cannot be thankful for an unpleasant situation such as divorce. Yet, if you read the story of Charlize Theron, you will realize that things could get much worse than separation. You only got divorced; no one died in the process! I do not mean any form of disrespect to Theron's family, yet, the reality is that some situations are more tragic than others. The fact that your spouse left you, does not mean that your life has ended. No matter what happens, there is always a positive angle to it if you are willing to explore that line of thought.

Pick The Lessons

Another way to take the sting out of a traumatic experience is by finding the lessons in it. One of the mistakes some people make is that they take the wrong lessons from their experiences. For example, instead of realizing that they were gullible to have believed someone who was obviously lying to them, they rather conclude that it is wrong to trust anyone.

That conclusion is not reasonable because there is no way we can relate to others without trusting them . What you should rather consider is your trust process. It is best that you do not trust people without testing them first. However, claiming that you will never trust anyone again, will not help you or the people around you. Learn the right things for a better future and recovery.

Focus On Your Present Reality

It is sad to discover that some people will never focus on their present reality. Even when their lives are moving in the right direction, they remain stuck in the past. If you are in a new relationship, there is no point in talking about an ex that brutally assaulted you. Your new partner might empathize with you initially but it will become problematic if you keep harping on it.

Let it go! Focus on your new relationship and make the best out of it. If you once had an abusive boss, forget about that chapter of your life when you get a new role. Painting your former boss black in front of your new employer, might make him or her see you as a disloyal person. So, let the new reality overwhelm your past.

Share Your Story

The moment you can laugh about your past, you have taken out its sting. When people are still hurting, they tend to be silent about their past experiences. However, when they heal from it, they are willing to share their experience as a lesson for others. Sharing your experience might bring back the pain of the memory at first, but over time, you will find out that the pain is gone.

This process will help you heal slowly because you will find people that will help you with different perspectives as you share your experience with them. The new perspectives can give you the much-needed paradigm shift that will help you heal from your past hurt.

Chapter Six:
Watch Out For The Triggers

"A lot of people who have experienced trauma at the hands of people they've trusted take responsibility, and that is what's toxic."

Hanah Gadsby

Indeed, traumatic events are stressful. What really makes things worse is the action of people around us. In some cases, these people are close to you, while in other cases, you find them online. Some individuals are professional bullies, if there is such a thing as that. It is in your best interest to avoid such people as you recover from traumatic events. This topic is the focal point of this chapter.

Never Forget The Lessons

Forgiveness is paramount. Regardless of how a person has hurt you, it is essential that you forgive them. You do not need to forgive others for their sake but because you need it. You will struggle to have inner peace and tranquility when you have people you hate in your life. So, what is best is that you forgive the people that hurt you for the sake of your own mental health.

Nonetheless, you will be making a huge mistake if you do not put measures in place that can help you prevent a repeat of such occurrences. You can tell that you have forgiven a person when you notice the following signs:

You Do Not Resent Them

Resentment is a natural product of being hurt. It is normal that you will have the urge to hate people that hurt you, especially when you trusted them but they betrayed you. So, the fact that you resent such people is to be expected.

Yet, it is best that you do not allow bitterness to overwhelm you because it can lead to disastrous outcomes. For example, you might want to hurt them in return, which can lead you into a life of crime. Therefore, it is advisable that you let go of the hurt to heal yourself. It is not the easiest of choices, but it is always what will be best for you.

You Do Not Wish The Person Evil

When people hurt us, we naturally want justice. We hope that they will be arrested and made to pay for their crimes. However, it is not always that simple. Sometimes, the legal system fails to punish them, and we are hurt even further.

We hope karma will help out but it might be taking too long, according to our estimation. In most cases, bad people get what they deserve but it is best that you do not wish them evil. When you want a person to experience a tragic occurrence because they have hurt you, you will be bitter, which is not good for your mental health.

You Do Not Rejoice At Their Downfall

In some cases, the people that hurt us get what they deserve. Yet, it is not best that we rejoice at their downfall and suffering. For example, if a person that cheated you is battling cancer, it will be inhumane of you to be glad that they are suffering.

As fellow human beings, we ought to be compassionate and empathetic towards each other. The fact that they hurt us should not turn us into monsters. You need this approach to life for your personal healing. Bitterness or cynicism is never the solution.

You Are Willing To Help Them When Necessary

No one should make you lose your humane values, such as compassion and empathy. You have not moved on from a traumatic event if you cannot imagine helping the person that hurt you. If someone wants to assassinate them, will you report it to the police?

If they seek employment in your company, will you help them? Refuse to let bitterness overwhelm you. It clouds your judgment and makes you prone to making mistakes. It is never worth it.

Common Triggers

As long as you have things around you that remind you of your past, it may be difficult to leave your past behind. Below are some prevalent triggers that make people stuck in their past:

Negative People

As long as you have people that enjoy negativity, you will continue to dwell in the past. Some individuals only get close to you during your low times to identify with you, especially when they have been through the same things. Instead of plotting how you can get out of the issue and focus on the future, they will want you to remain in that rut with them.

If you do not stay away from such people, they will influence you with their negativity and make you hate the world as they do. They want you to embrace their worldview of negativity as a form of consolation and solace for their dilemma. It is, therefore, best that you avoid such people.

Staying In The Same Environment

It might be difficult to recover from a traumatic experience if you remain in the same location where it occurred. For example, if you lose your loved ones at the hands of a criminal group in your area, remaining in that place might put you at risk and make you fearful of a recurrence of that event.

Therefore, in such cases, a relocation might be best for you. Of course, this rule does not apply to every traumatic experience. Yet, a change of environment after a traumatic event is an effective way of giving yourself the space to heal and get your life back on track.

Sticking With The Same Person

Many people underestimate the pain that comes from staying around a person that hurts them. For example, a woman staying with an abusive husband is risking a lot. If Charlize Theron's mother had left the home at the height of the abuse, she could have avoided being forced to kill a man she once loved, in front of her daughter.

No one should be allowed to push you against the wall. Even if you kill them out of self-defense, the fact remains that you have murdered someone, which will remain with you for the rest of your life. Charlize Theron can never forget that experience! It is always best to stay away from your source of trauma as far as possible.

Secretly Missing Them

Sometimes, while remembering a person we once loved, we only recall all the good times we had with them and ignore all the bad things. Consequently, we secretly miss them and wish we were with them still. Eventually, we reconnect with them and they hurt us again.

The wound is opened afresh and we are traumatized again. Never forget the reasons you chose to distance yourself from a person in the first place. It will help you to avoid reconnecting with them in time, and to have them so hurt you again.

Chapter Seven:
It's Victory Time!

"It is only in sorrow that bad weather masters us; in joy, we face the storm and defy it."

Amelia Barr

Victory is a priceless commodity. It is the product of the investment of effort, time, energy, and other resources to achieve the desired result. In this chapter, we will delve deeper into proven tactics that can help transform you from a victim into a champion in your journey toward recovery. It is time to win!

Practical Steps To Practice For Healing

Breathing exercises and the use of positive affirmations are two exceptional tools you can use to recover from traumatic events.

Breathing Exercises

You can practice breathing exercises by following the steps below:

- Ensure you are wearing a comfortable outfit.

- Sit comfortably in a place where you have few distractions.

- Inhale deeply, such that your breath flows deeply into your belly, comfortably, without force.

- Ensure that you are breathing through your nose instead of your mouth.

- Breathe in gently and enjoy the soothing feeling of the experience. Ensure that your mind is not wandering as you do this.

- Breathe out in such a way that the air flows out gently as you count from 1 to 5.

You can repeat the process as often as needed. This exercise comes in handy whenever the thoughts of the past threaten to make you incandescent with rage and bitterness.

Positive Affirmations

The words you speak have a way of affecting your thoughts and emotions. So, by saying positive things, you can heal gradually from past hurts. The following steps can help you practice positive affirmations:

- Identify the positive correlation of your negative thoughts.

- Write them out somewhere you can see them in your home or office.

- Speak those words audibly.

- Repeat the process as many times as possible during the day.

Chase Your Dreams

One of the best ways you can move on from traumatic events is by chasing your dreams. What are those things you have always wanted to do with your life that had been prevented because of the experience? It is time to get back to them. The following tips will help you in this respect:

State The Vision Again

Your experiences can threaten to change your perception of yourself. Who says you cannot succeed just because you had a traumatic childhood? Of course, it is all in your head! What matters most is what you think of yourself and not the opinion of other people. If Will Smith, Oprah Winfrey, and others could turn their lives around despite their traumatic childhood, then you can also have a glorious future.

Now is the time to start sowing the seeds that will germinate in the future for you.

Your past does not define you. It is all about what you want for yourself and your willingness to pay the price. You can either become a victor or remain a victim of your circumstances. It is time to restate your vision. Bring out those dreams and plans you had before the trauma. Your story has not ended. It is time to start writing new chapters. You were born a giant; circumstances should not make you settle for less. The ball is in your court. Strike it hard!

Set Goals

Research has discovered a strong link between setting goals and focusing. Setting goals is an attribute that is prevalent among achievers. If you do not know your destination, you cannot identify your distraction. However, when you determine what you want to achieve in your life, you can consciously work towards it. In the process of working towards achieving your goals, you will realize that the traumatic event only threatened to derail you.

Your trauma should not turn you into a monster. Rather, it should be a source of fuel for you to do better things. Let the setback and pain inspire you to show the world that achieving success is possible, regardless of adversity and setbacks. When you read the stories of the people we mentioned earlier, what you will discover is that they made up their minds to make the best of their lives, regardless of their previous experiences.

Believe In Yourself

If you do not trust yourself, no one will. It is the degree to which you trust yourself that others will be willing to consider you for something important. For example, no one would vote you in as the president of the US if you do not believe you have what it takes to take the nation from its current level to a higher level. Self-confidence is contagious and attractive. When you have a dream you believe in and are committed to, people will eventually join you in achieving it.

It all begins by believing in yourself. People love leaders that know where they are going and have created clear paths for others to follow. So, it is critical that you have a clear path in life. Redefine yourself based on your goals and not based on your past. There are endless opportunities in life for self-confident people that are willing to strive to achieve greatness.

Acquire Skills

Setting goals and believing in yourself is not enough to help you achieve success. Rather, they serve as a springboard that will inspire you to make the right choices. One of the things you need to do to improve yourself and give yourself a chance to succeed is the acquisition of skills.

It can come in the form of enrolling yourself in an institution or a skill acquisition center, where you will receive a certificate. The modern world is full of many unconventional roles, such as social media manager, software engineer, human resources management, data analysis, etc. So, you can always find something you love. Once you do, give it your best and banish the demons of your past.

Invest In Yourself

There are various aspects of your life, such as your career, relationships , spiritual, and social life. According to the World Health Organization, a person is deemed to be healthy when they have their social, emotional, and physical state under control. So, building up yourself goes beyond a commitment to your career.

One of the reasons some people have a lopsided life is that they ignore other areas of their lives and only focus on certain aspects. Invest in every area of your life. Develop yourself spiritually, intellectually, socially, and in your interactions with others. The more you feel like you are growing and developing, the more you will enjoy your life and forget your past.

Chapter Eight:
Be Ruthless!

"What we change inwardly will change outer reality."

Plutarch

We all have reasons to be sentimental. Nonetheless, it is our approach to life that ends up limiting us. If you have identified your source of trauma, it is imperative that you are ruthless toward it. You might need to end some relationships or limit the access some people have to you to cut out their influence over you. A new life requires ruthlessness, and this discussion is the crux of the next chapter.

Go For It!

One of the reasons the divorce rate in the modern world is outlandish is the tendency of people to ignore red flags. Of course, you cannot marry a perfect person because such a person does not exist. Yet, it is not advisable to overlook behaviors that you cannot tolerate in marriage, during the courtship period. This lack of ruthlessness sows the seed of broken homes. Miracles do not take place within marriages. On the contrary, it gives people the freedom to express their true nature.

For example, men do not become abusive overnight. If you are in a relationship with a person that has the tendency to emotionally and physically abuse others, he will do it to you someday. The fact that he is kind to you because you are in love is not enough. Is he kind toward others? Is he rude or respectful when speaking to his friends and family? You cannot afford to ignore such ominous signs. If you do, you will pay dearly for it in the future.

If you are not ruthless in your decisions, you are prone to repeating your past mistakes. The chance that you will experience another traumatic event is high when you have this approach to life. It is best to take your time to find the kind of job that suits you or someone that truly cares about you, instead of jumping into every opportunity. This approach will only lead to years of instability and wasting of time.

How To Be Ruthless In Your Decision

If you have never been ruthless in your past, you might find it challenging to approach life with this new approach. Yet, it is exactly what you need to prevent a repeat of traumatic events. Below are some tips that can help you in this respect:

Count the Cost

Sentimental decisions will cost you a lot in different ways. It can cost you your career or marriage. So, before you allow yourself to overlook things instead of dealing with them decisively, think about the cost.

Successful businesspeople are some of the most ruthless people in the world. They do not hire people based on sentiments and do not allow their friends and families to take their business for granted. Sometimes, it makes some people hate them or call them stingy, but they know that they need to be like that to succeed in business.

It is vital that you treat others the way you want to be treated. For example, if you value your loved ones, pay them, and expect the same standard from them if they work for you. Do not create room for sentiment because they can come back to haunt you. If someone is overstepping their boundaries in your life, make it clear to them that you do not want such behavior to continue. It will set a precedent for others. Always remember that sentimental decisions can be costly. It will keep you on your toes.

Remember The Pain

Have you regretted a sentimental decision in the past? Do you wish you had cut off a relationship earlier? Do you wish you had quit the job before it tarnished your reputation? Of course, you do not have to experience the pain that comes with making sentimental decisions before you avoid it. Yet, if you have experienced the anguish that comes with living this way, it is a gift from above.

It will teach you to do what you need to do to avoid grave consequences. People can be wicked and brutal when you give them the opportunity to hurt you. No amount of apologies can ameliorate the pain that comes from being hurt by the people you trust. Therefore, ruthlessness is a weapon that should never be missing from your arsenal. If you give a person an opportunity and they misuse it, take note. Unless you see a remarkable change in attitude, you will be making a huge mistake by giving them similar opportunities in the future.

Consider The Effort Of Others

If some people put in the effort and invest their time to help you recover from a traumatic event, they will be hugely disappointed in you if they see you making the same mistake again. If you were brutalized by a man you loved as a woman, leading to trauma, it is unwise to trust that person again. Apart from the likely pain that comes from making such moves, you will also disappoint the people that did their best to help you recover.

It is unfair to undo the good works of others, and they will likely ignore you if you get into trouble again. One of the reasons you need to be ruthless is that it shows that you value the investment of others in your life. In a cold world where many people do not care about others, if you find people willing to make sacrifices for your welfare, you should appreciate it.

If you don't, they will be disappointed, and it might set the wrong precedent for the future. The moment your loved ones consider you stoic in pursuing the same person or circumstances, things will only grow worse from that point on.

Remember How Far You Have Come

Some people have a culture of forgetting their pain, once they heal from trauma. They forget the sleepless nights and the days they cried bitterly, once they are in a good place again. Of course, forgiveness is therapeutic. Yet, you cannot afford to forget the lessons. If you give people an inch, they will take a yard. Your life is not some kind of experiment to find out how much pain you can withstand.

Get hold of your life and set boundaries. Everyone close to you should know what they can do when they are around you and the lines they cannot cross. It is a simple but effective technique for living a happy life. Always remember what it took to get you to where you are. You cannot afford to go back to those days when you were miserable and hated yourself because of what someone did to you. It is time to set standards for yourself and run your life in the way that is best for you.

Chapter Nine:
Tell The Tales

"Self-confidence is contagious."

Stephen Richard

Dead men tell no tales! Well, you did not die in the course of battling your trauma! Congratulations! You are a survivor. One of the reasons you should be motivated to overcome traumatic events is that your story will be a source of inspiration to others. There are people in the world today that are discouraged to the point of contemplating suicide.

What such people need is a ray of hope – a survivor of a similar experience. In the words of Jesus Christ to Peter, who would deny him, "and when you have returned to Me, strengthen your brethren." In the same way, after you have survived and recovered from a traumatic event, let your story encourage others and inspire them not to give up. This discussion is the focal point of this final chapter.

Create A Blog

Creating a blog is one of the best ways you can tell your story. The reality is that many people are looking for hope in this dark, cold world. When you begin to tell your story, you will realize that there are so many people battling the same issue that will find a ray of hope in how you navigated your way out of a setback. I love to read the stories of victors. They inspire me to realize that the mission is possible!

Your blog will serve the dual purpose of giving people hope and also serving as a source of income. It is best that you learn how to package your story in such a way that people will look forward to the next time you are creating a post. Of course, you do not have to add any form of falsehood to the story to make it sensational or inspiring. Make it simple and sincere but exciting and inspiring.

Write A Book

More people seem to prefer to read e-books in recent times, but books can never be outdated. They are priceless gifts that inform, inspire, entertain, and build us up. Unlike writing blogs, you can be more deliberate with your planning when you write a book. As you compile your manuscript, you can always remove parts you feel are not relevant and replace them with more useful details.

This is one of the ways you can both tell your story and earn a profit. An example of such a book is *Gifted Hands* by Dr. Ben Carson. One of my friends that read the book made up his mind that he would become a surgeon, against all the odds! It was a book that inspired many people around the world. Well, while the world was getting inspiration and reason to dream, the famous surgeon was also smiling all the way to the bank.

YouTube Channel

New YouTube videos are springing up by the day because people have discovered that it is a quick way to achieve fame while earning money. If you have interesting content, this vlog platform can catapult you into global recognition in no time. Some people have millions of subscribers on YouTube. It is all a function of your ability to create the kind of content that people love to see.

Of course, nothing is more exciting than the stories of people that recovered from adversity and made the most of their lives. So, if you leverage this platform to tell your story, it will reinstate your confidence and you will also inspire other people around the world battling similar challenges. Additionally, it is also a way to monetize your victory over trauma.

Start A TV Show

If you are the kind of person that is comfortable with presenting in front of cameras, a TV show might be what you need to share your story. Of course, this is not as easy as others. However, if you have what it takes to leverage this platform, take advantage of it to tell others about your journey from trauma back to a normal life. Even if you cannot run a TV show by yourself, embrace opportunities to appear on such programs.

There are many people around the world that would love to see people that understand their pain. When they hear you, they will be inspired to keep pushing and believing that they can recover from such setbacks. It is one of the ways you can make the world a better place. It also comes with privileges, such as endorsements and access to important people.

Present On The Radio

Radio platforms might not be as popular as they used to be, especially among the younger generation. Yet, they remain great platforms for reaching a large audience. If your story is inspiring enough, more people will listen to the program because recovery stories are always worthwhile.

People will, directly or indirectly, pick up tips from what you say and implement them in their lives. I am sure you will be happy when you find out that your story was the reason many people around the world refused to give up on themselves. Only a few people can say they have achieved such feats.

My Final Words

You might not be able to determine your experiences in life. Sometimes, we experience sad events due to our mistakes but that is not always the case. In some cases, it is the people we trust the most, such as our parents, friends, and family members that expose us to torturous events that threaten to change our lives forever.

Yet, you can always determine what you choose to do with those experiences. All through this journey, I have encouraged you to make lemonades with those lemons. It is literally the only option you have to put your life back on track.

Other options, such as hating the perpetrators and taking revenge, will only turn you into a monster. It is time to start facing the facts. Take matters into your hands and take advantage of this material to recover. You can still make the best of your life if only you choose to. You are superbly and irrevocably loved by me! Today is still a good day to be alive!

References

Bardes, M., and Piccolo, R. F. (2010). "Goal setting as an antecedent of destructive leader behaviors" in *When Leadership Goes Wrong: Destructive Leadership, Mistakes, and Ethical Failures*. Eds. B. Schyns and T. Hansbrough (Charlotte, NC: IAP Information Age Publishing), 3–22.

Forgiveness: Your Health Depends on It. (2020). Johns Hopkins Medicine. Retrieved September 22, 2021, from https://www.hopkinsmedicine.org/health/wellness-and-prevention/forgiveness-your-health-depends-on-it

Long, K.N.G., Worthington, E.L., VanderWeele, T.J., et al. Forgiveness of others and subsequent health and well-being in mid-life: a longitudinal *study on female nurses. BMC Psychol 8, 104*

(2020). https://doi.org/10.1186/s40359-020-00470-w

World Health Organisation (2021). *Depression.*
https://www.who.int/health-topics/depression

Wilkinson and Finkbeiner (2022). Divorce Statistics: Over 115 Studies, Facts and Rates for 2022. Available at: https://www.wf-lawyers.com/divorce-statistics-and-facts/

Thank you for reading this book!

If you found this book helpful, I would be grateful if you would **post an honest review on Amazon** so this book can reach other supportive readers like you!

All you need to do is digitally flip to the back and leave your review. Or visit amazon.com/author/senseipauldavid click the correct book cover and click on the blue link next to the yellow stars that say, "customer reviews."

As always...
It's a great day to be alive!

Get/Share Our FREE All-Ages Mental Health Book Now!

FREE Self-Development Book for Every Family

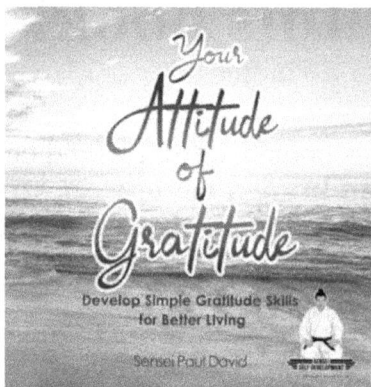

senseiselfdevelopment.senseipublishing.com

Click Below or Search Amazon for Another Book In This Series Or Visit:

www.amazon.com/author/senseipauldavid

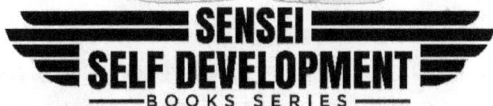

SENSEI
SELF DEVELOPMENT
BOOKS SERIES

senseiselfdevelopment.senseipublishing.com

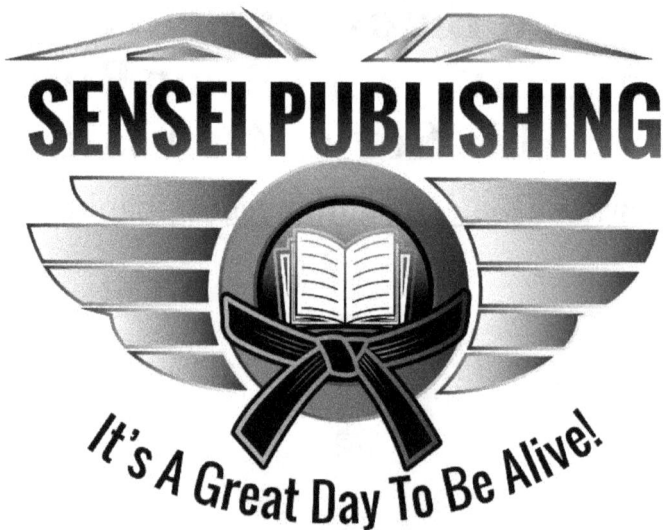

Join Our Publishing Journey!

If you would like to receive FREE BOOKS, and special offers, please visit www.senseipublishing.com and join our newsletter by entering your email address in the pop-up box

Follow Our Engaging Blog NOW! senseipauldavid.ca

Get Our FREE Books Today!

Click & Share the Link Below

FREE Self-Development Book
senseiselfdevelopment.senseipublishing.com

FREE BONUS!!!
Experience Over 25 FREE Engaging Guided
Meditations!

Prized Skills & Practices for Adults & Kids.
Help Restore Deep Sleep, Lower Stress,
Improve Posture, Navigate Uncertainty &
More.

Download the Free Insight Timer App and click the link
below:
http://insig.ht/sensei_paul

About Sensei Publishing

Sensei Publishing commits itself to helping people of all ages transform into better versions of themselves by providing high-quality and research-based self-development books with an emphasis on mental health and guided meditations. Sensei Publishing offers well-written e-books, audiobooks, paperbacks and online courses that simplify complicated but practical topics in line with its mission to inspire people towards positive transformation.

It's a great day to be alive!

About the Author

I create simple & transformative eBooks & Guided Meditations for Adults & Children proven to help navigate uncertainty, solve niche problems & bring families closer together.

I'm a former finance project manager, private pilot, jiu-jitsu instructor, musician & former University of Toronto Fitness Trainer. I prefer a science-based approach to focus on these & other areas in my life to stay humble & hungry to evolve. I hope you enjoy my work and I'd love to hear your feedback.

- It's a great day to be alive!
Sensei Paul David

Scan & Follow/Like/Subscribe: Facebook, Instagram,
YouTube: @senseipublishing

Scan using your phone/iPad camera for Social Media
Visit us at www.senseipublishing.com and sign up for
our newsletter to learn more about our exciting books
and to experience our FREE Guided Meditations for
Kids & Adults.